Phegal

4/6

THEN AND THERE SERIES

GENERAL EDITOR

MARJORIE REEVES, M.A., Ph.D.

Prehistoric Britain

ROBIN PLACE, M.A.

Illustrated from contemporary sources by

ANN HOPKINS

LONGMANS

LONGMANS, GREEN AND CO LTD
48, Grosvenor Street, London W.1.
*Associated companies, branches and representatives
throughout the world*

*First published 1959
Second impression 1960
Fifth impression 1966
Sixth impression 1968*

Cover design by
Peter Pickard, A.R.C.A., M.S.I.A.

Printed in Hong Kong by Peninsula Press Ltd.

CONTENTS

ON THE PLAIN AND THE DOWNS

THE wind blows strong across the chalk uplands of Salisbury Plain. The rolling hills, covered with short sheep-cropped grass, stretch for miles, and only occasional beech-woods break the smooth line of the horizon and offer a barrier to the wind.

Salisbury Plain and the Marlborough Downs together form a great chalk block, thirty miles from north to south and fifty miles from east to west. Find a map of this part of England. Do you see how few towns and villages there are? Thousands of years ago, when England was just beginning to be settled by wandering tribes, more people lived on Salisbury Plain than in most of the rest of England. The low-lying land and the river valleys were marshy and covered with dense woods too thick to be cleared by the stone axes of prehistoric men. But movement was easy on the lightly-wooded dry chalk uplands. In the white chalk, too, there were flints to make their tools and their weapons.

If you visit these chalk-lands today, you will find them very much the same as in prehistoric days.

You may still see the marks of an ancient trackway leading over the hills down to a distant river. You will see the huge ditches and ramparts of a hill-top camp and the mounds which mark ancient burying-places. If you search you may be lucky enough to find a flint arrowhead or some flint tool. The great stone temples at Avebury and Stonehenge are the most amazing monuments left by these early men. As you read of how the stones were brought there and arranged in great circles, perhaps you will be able to picture the busy scene at the temple and all around the rolling hills, and the grass and bright flowers dancing in the breeze.

NEW STONE AGE FARMERS

The Round-up at Windmill Hill

IT was a very hot day, far too hot for digging. The boy wondered whether he could slip away to the stream for a drink without being seen. His father's back was turned, but he decided that he would be sure to be seen as he ran down the hill and it was far too hot for a beating. When his father turned round, the boy had picked up his digging tool again and was hard at work. This is his tool. It was made from the *antler** of a red deer and was about two feet long. The point had to be hammered into the chalk with a stone, then levered backwards and forwards until the chalk was loosened. It was very hard work. When a pile of broken chalk lay at the bottom of the pit, the boy scooped it up in his shovel and put it into a leather sack. When the sack was full, he scrambled out of the pit and emptied it on a big heap of chalk.

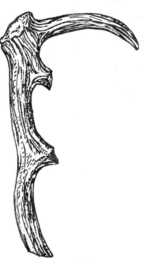

Antler pick

* You will find words printed like *this* in the Glossary on pages 91–92.

I

His shovel was made of the flat shoulder-blade of an ox tied on to the end of a stick with a leather *thong*. As you

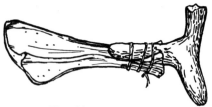

Shoulder-blade shovel

can see in the picture, it was not very broad, but it was better than scooping up the chalk in his hands.

He was working on top of a hill, along with a crowd of people all busy making a cattle camp. Three circular banks of earth were being thrown up, one inside the other, round the highest part of the hill. This would leave a grassy space on the very top. The banks were made of chalk dug out of ditches. The camp, with its banks and deep ditches, was not meant to keep human enemies out but to keep cattle in. Once the animals were driven into the space at the very top of the hill, through the gaps left across the ditches and the banks, hurdles were put across these gaps and then they could not get out again. Here is a plan of the camp.

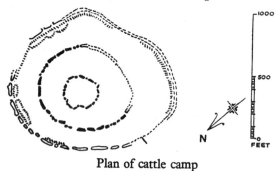

Plan of cattle camp

The boy remembered how every year his *clan* met many other clans, all with their cattle, to make a camp on top of a hill like this one. They always met in the autumn, before the winter came on, when there were plenty of berries and wild fruit of all kinds to eat. For the rest of the year they split up, so that each group could have its own grazing lands.

If you ask why they went to all this trouble in digging ditches and making banks, the answer is that this was the only way of keeping all the cattle together once they had been rounded up. You will see in a moment what they did with the cattle when they were gathered inside the banks.

It was windy on the hill. When the sun set, the people stopped their work. Each family found a deep pit for shelter to sleep in. Here is one where people used to live.

A home in a cattle camp ditch

3

They lit a fire, and cooked their meat over it—sometimes one of their own bullocks, sometimes an animal that one of them had trapped, or shot with bow and arrow. The arrowheads they used were made of thin, sharp *flint*. The picture below shows what the arrowhead looked like. To make one, little pieces of flint were pressed off each side with a hard bone. You can see in the picture the marks left where the little pieces of flint came off. An arrowhead was only about one inch long. The one in the picture is drawn larger to show you how it was made.

Flint arrowhead

When each family finished gnawing their bones, they threw them down by the fire. Gradually these bones became buried in the chalky dirt, with pieces of stone that flew about when flint was being chipped into tools round the fire (1)*.

The boy was very glad indeed when, after many days, the digging finished. His hands were red and blistered, and he was very tired of hacking away at the chalk.

* You will find out how we know this by looking up this number on page 87. Look up each number as you come to it.

At last the work of rounding up the cattle began. The herds had been kept together by children while the camp was being dug. Now the cattle were driven up the hill and guided across the gaps in the ditches. It was very noisy and exciting. The men shouted, and the dogs (2) barked to keep the animals going in the right direction. Sometimes a cow broke loose, and careered bellowing across the grass. Sometimes a young animal was pushed over the edge into a deep ditch, and had to be slaughtered there and then. Finally they were all inside, and the barriers of hurdles were put across the gaps.

The boy kept close to his father as they pushed their way among the frightened animals. All the men and boys were sorting the cattle. It was an important task. All summer the cattle found grass to eat, but in the winter there was very little food for them. Only a few of the best animals could be kept alive, so that a new herd could be bred from them in the spring. The rest of the young animals had now to be slaughtered (3). Here is the skull of a slaughtered bullock.

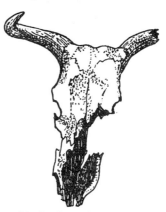

The dead animals were at once handed over to the women and girls, who skinned them. They used sharp flint knives to take out *sinews* to

Skull of a young cow

serve as string, and split the leg bones. There was plenty to eat then. With the thought of the winter before them, everyone ate as much as possible while the meat lasted. In the coming months, there would be only the stock cattle

5

for breeding. These could not be killed and eaten, or there would be no cattle at all next year. So the clans would depend for food on hunting, and on their precious stores of grain.

The boy slipped away from the dust to visit his mother and sisters. They were busy cleaning the skins of the slaughtered beasts. His favourite sister, who was just a little older than he was, held out a scraper. He threw it back at her. "Woman's work!" he said, proudly brandishing his herding stick. She laughed at him, and went on scraping the fat off the inside of the skin. This is her scraper.

A flint scraper

"It's lucky you've got women to work for you," she said. "Otherwise, where would your clothes come from?"

"I don't need any more," he said. Stooping down, he picked up one of her tools. "What's this for?" he asked.

"It takes the hair off the outside of the skin, when I've soaked it. It's made of deer antler."

An antler skin-comb

6

"I can see that," replied her brother. "But what a dull job!"

"It isn't," said the girl. "I like to feel the skin getting soft as I work on it, and wonder which of us will wear it. If you'll make me some new scrapers, I'll ask mother to let you have this one, and make it extra soft for you. You will be glad to wrap yourself up in it by the fire when the nights are cold."

The boy was feeling tired after all the excitement of sorting the cattle. He remembered a big lump of flint he had noticed sticking out of the bank of one of the ditches. He had hurt his toe on it when sliding down to watch some men dealing with a bullock that had fallen in.

He went off, and presently came back with pieces of the stone, which he had smashed to get some chips of the right size. He squatted down on the grass, battering the edge of each flint with a hammerstone.

Their mother shouted to the younger children to go and fetch water and sticks for the fire.

"It's the last time!" she said to another woman. "My man has finished his work, and we have many skins ready for the cold days to come."

The boy and girl felt sad. They enjoyed the round-up. It was fun meeting all the people from other clans. Once the meeting was over, they would go back to their wandering life with their own clan. In the long winter to come they would very often be cold and hungry.

"Come on," said the girl, jumping up suddenly. "I found some lovely nuts down by the stream, and if we don't hurry up someone else will eat the lot."

The children ran off down the hill, into the cool of the woods, looking for hazel nuts.

7

The Traders

One of the women in the clan was different from all the rest. She was taller, and had strange ways. Her people were the traders, who travelled about exchanging axes of specially hard stone and deer antlers, for flour. She had stayed behind, after one of their visits, to marry the boy's eldest brother.

When her people had gone away she had been very sad. At first the girls in her new tribe laughed at her, for she did not know how to make pottery or grind corn into flour. But in the end they admired her strength. She was able to work for hours without tiring, and was cleverer than they were at snaring animals and finding things to eat in the woods. And she was very clever at curing skins.

She was surprised to see the clay pots which the other women used. She told them how her people carried water in leather bottles and made other containers of bark. The women argued about which was better—to make clay pots, which took a long time, and were easily broken, or to use leather ones.

Then they taught the newcomer how to make clay pots. They showed her the best places to look for clay. It had to be mixed with grit, or finely-crushed pieces of broken pot, so that the pot would not crack when it was being fired. To make a pot the woman squatted on the ground and rolled handfuls of clay into long rolls between the palms of her hands. Then she built up the pot by coiling the rolls round and round. As she worked, she smoothed the sides of the pot, to hide the joins between the coils. The bottom of the pot was always rounded, not flat. This made it less likely to be upset when put down on the uneven ground. Sometimes a woman would stand her pot on a mat made of reeds (4) while she was shaping it. If she stood it on the ground, bits of rubbish like odd grains of corn (5) became mixed with the wet clay.

In return for lessons in pot-making, the strange woman taught the others to make baskets.

One day the traders arrived on another visit. The strange woman's mother was among them again. The traders spread out on the ground the things they wished to trade to the farmers. There was a great pile of deer antlers. The farmers needed these for digging. There were two different heaps of stone. One heap was of flint, pieces of black, glassy stone. The traders mined this themselves from deep in the earth. The farmers knew that it was easier to shape than the flint they picked up themselves on the surface of the ground. It was less brittle, too, because it had not lain in the hot sun and cold frost, and so the tools they made from it did not break so easily.

The other heap of stone was made up of lumps of very hard rock, roughly shaped into the form of axes. This rock was quite different from any other stone the boy had seen. It was greenish, not at all like flint, and he knew that it could not be chipped into shape like a flint axe. If his father needed a new axe for cutting down trees he would exchange flour for a lump of this rock. Then he would give it to the boy to grind until it was smooth and polished, with a sharp edge.

9

This meant crouching on the ground in front of a big stone with a flat surface, on which the lump of rock was rubbed up and down until it became smooth. This is the stone the boy used. The rubbing wore grooves in it. It

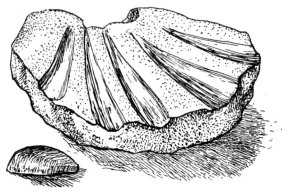

Stone for grinding axes

was very hard work. You can find out for yourselves how difficult it was. Try making a big stone smooth by rubbing it on a rock. The boy used to sprinkle sand from the stream on the stone, as it made the job a little quicker. Although he could make a flint axe in a few minutes when his father needed one, the rock axe would last much longer once it was finished, for it never broke as the flint one did.

"Where do you find the axe-rock?" the boy asked one of the traders. The trader waved his hand towards the west. "When we travel towards the setting sun, we come at last to mountains. They are much higher than the hills on which you drive your cattle in the autumn, and there are no trees on them. In places that we know of, where none of you corn-people live, we find the strong axe-rock.

Some mountains are green, like this rock. Others are pink and grey, and sparkle (6) in the sun as if they were made of stars."

"Do you dig it out of the mountain with deer antlers, as we dig our chalk ditches?" asked the boy, curiously.

The man laughed loudly. "We should break all the antlers we ever collected doing that. No, we explore the slopes of the mountains looking for heaps of stones. These are cracked off the mountain by winter frost and snow. Rain washes them down the sides of the mountain into great piles. When we find such a pile, we camp near it, and look at all the broken rock. We choose all the pieces that are the right size for axes, and batter them into roughly the right shape. Then they are ready for boys like you to grind smooth on a grinding-stone."

"But how do you shape this rock?" asked the boy. "I can never shape it with my flint axe. I used to try, but it only broke the edge of my axe."

"Our hammers are made of rock just as hard as the axe-rock," the man replied. "They are very big and heavy, and though they cannot make a sharp edge, they make the lumps of rock roughly axe-shaped, and save us carrying waste stone."

Meanwhile the woman who had married the boy's brother had found her mother among the traders and was eagerly telling her all the new ways she had learned. She showed her mother how to grind corn into soft white flour between two stones, and then gave her some of the flat cakes she had cooked in the ashes of the fire.

"We may not be able to do all these new things that you have learned," said the girl's mother finally, "but I will show you something that we have learned. On our last visit, we saw the women making grey earth into hard round

Pot made by a trader's wife

things that held water without running out. If we put water into our baskets it all runs away. So we watched the women at work, and went away and made some of these pots. Here is one, to show you that you are not the only one who can learn new ways."

She held out something she had wrapped in a skin. The girl took it and laughed. "It looks just the same as a basket. Our pots are never covered with a pattern all over like this. They are smooth."

Her mother looked cross. "But we are used to having baskets, and this must look like what we are used to. That is why I make a pattern on any pot I make. It takes a long time. I take a piece of string made of twisted plant stems, and loop it round my finger. When I press the loop all over the wet clay, it leaves a pattern that makes the pot look like one of the baskets I have made all my life."

"It looks as though the pot were covered with maggots," (7) said the girl, and ran her hand over one of her own smooth pots.

Pot made by a farmer's wife

The farmers had done their trading, and the men were talking together as the traders packed up their goods. The boy's father called him.

"Would you like to travel with the traders? We have taken one of their girls into our family, and, if you like, they will take you with them for a journey. They are going to get the dark flint-stone."

The boy was excited at the thought of a journey with the traders, but disappointed that they were not going to the axe-rock mountains.

"You will not climb mountains if you come with us this time," said the trader, who seemed to know what the boy was thinking. "But wait till you see our flint-mines! We will go deep under the earth to find the flint. That is, unless you are afraid to come with us under the earth."

"Of course not," replied the boy quickly. "Do we go towards the sunset to see the flint-mines?"

"No! We go towards the sunrise. At dawn we will set off with the sun in our faces. You will not see the mountains of the sunset on this journey."

The Flint-Mines at Grimes Graves

It was a long way to the flint-mines and the boy lost count of the days. They travelled along the ridges of hills whenever they could. These were wooded, but there were not so many trees as in the valleys between the hills. When they had to cross a valley, the boy kept close to the man in front of him, so that the twigs and branches pushed aside by him did not lash back into the boy's face.

A 2—P.-H. B.   13

The undergrowth was thick, and his legs got very scratched.

Sometimes they had to swim across rivers. One of the girls showed the boy how to float across, clinging to a log and kicking with his legs. The boy learned to run quietly, and he and other children sometimes sped ahead of the loaded traders, to see if they could surprise timid deer drinking, or beavers at work building dams with trees that they had cut down with their sharp teeth.

At night they camped beside a large fire. The children did not stray far away in the dark, for they knew there were wolves and bears (8) prowling in the forest around them.

At last there were fewer hills to climb, and it was not many days before the traders met a band of men and women whom they knew well. They travelled together through the woods.

As they walked along, the boy cried out, for he had suddenly sunk into a patch of soft ground up to his knees. The trader pulled him out and laughed.

"You have fallen into one of the old *shafts*. We fill them up with the earth we take out when a new one is dug. You will soon notice that the ground looks different where a shaft has been filled up, and then you will learn to avoid it, as I do, without thinking about it. Tomorrow we will begin to dig our new shaft."

They stopped in a large clearing, and next day the trader, helped by the boy and another man and his daughter, marked out their shaft. It was to be round, about as wide across as three men lying down head to foot. Not far away was an old shaft. The trader told the boy to empty the chalk dug out of the new shaft into the old one. It was less trouble than piling up a big mound, and would

14

fill in a dangerous hole in the ground. This is what the shaft would look like when it was finished.

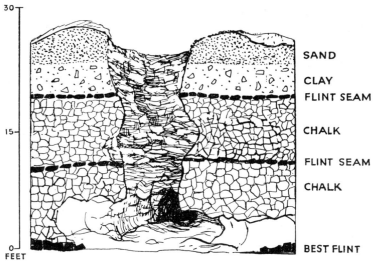

A section through a flint-mine shaft

At first digging was easy, as the ground was sandy. Then the boy found that as he dug he came to grey clay, which was harder to move. He did not fill the leather sack he was using so quickly now. "I wish our shaft was not so wide," he grumbled to the girl.

She was sitting on the ground twisting thongs of leather to make ropes. Beside her was a clay pot full of water. It was covered with patterns made by pressing small bird bones and a loop of cord against the wet clay pot before it was fired.

"Would you like a drink?" she asked.

The boy laid down his antler pick and stood upright.

"I would! I'll just fill up this sack, then I can empty it and have a drink before I get down again."

15

When he had dug out some more clay, he heaved the sack out of the shaft, which was about five feet deep. Then he scrambled up the side himself. He emptied the sack into the old shaft, and listened for the thump as the soil landed at the bottom. Then he sat down beside the girl. He dipped his hand into the jar to take out some water.

"That's better," he said, gratefully.

The two men came over to drink too. The girl's father tested the rope she was making, then sent her off to look for a branch to make a new handle for his shovel. The trader looked at the boy's part of the shaft.

"You dig quickly, but do not make the sides too straight. Let the shaft slope inwards. We have allowed for this in making it very wide at the top. If you make the sides straight, they may fall in on top of us. It is much safer to make them slope."

Early next morning the trader cut down a small tree. It took about ten minutes (9). Then the trader told the boy to fetch another axe and help him.

"We must make this into a ladder. The shaft is getting too deep to climb in and out of as we did yesterday. Chop off all the branches and twigs. Then cut notches in the tree-trunk as I do, but on the other side, and in between my notches."

When they had finished chopping, the tree-trunk had steps cut in it, on opposite sides. They rolled it to the side of the shaft, and lowered one end to the bottom. The boy was soon used to climbing up and down it.

That day the boy found his first piece of flint. It was lying at the top of the chalk, which was under the layer of clay that he had dug through. He picked it up, but was disappointed when the trader told him to throw it away.

"That is not good flint," he said. "There is better

16

below, so we do not waste time with that. Beneath this band of flint there is nothing but white chalk for a long way down. Then there is another band of flint. Beneath that there is more chalk, and then the layer of good stone we are looking for."

"Then we stop digging," said the boy.

"No, then we start digging!" said the trader, laughing. "Instead of digging downwards, we follow the flint along the ground as far as it is safe. We make tunnels in the chalk for a long way." These are some tunnels made by flint miners.

At the bottom of a flint-mine shaft

"But isn't it dark?" asked the boy.

"I will show you how to make a chalk lamp (10). We fill our lamps with animal fat, and a wick. They make a lot of smoke, like a fire, but they give us light to see the flint." There is a picture of a lamp on this page.

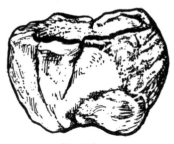

Chalk lamp

It was many days of hard digging before the flint-miners found the layer of flint that they were looking for. The boy knew when he had come to it. He was breaking away lumps of chalk by hammering the point on his pick into a crack in the chalk with a stone. Suddenly a lump broke away with a crack. Where it broke, it was black and very shiny. It had a white crust, made by chemicals in the white chalk staining the outside of the black flint.

The trader was very pleased to see the thick, black flint. Levering out blocks of chalk at different places on the floor, he showed the boy how the black flint spread all over the bottom of the shaft. Soon they had cleared all the chalk above the flint. The girl's father kept hauling up the sacks on the rope she had made, until the flint was uncovered. Then the trader shouted up to him that the next load would be flint. If he had not been told, he might have tipped the precious load down the old shaft with the chalk rubble!

The flint broke away in great pieces. The trader used several deer-antler picks at once. He hammered them into weak places in the layer of stone, then told the boy to press some in one direction or another, while he pulled on others.

That evening, as bats (11) were flying among the trees, a party of miners sat together in an old shaft that gave them shelter from the wind. They had made a fire in the shaft to keep them warm.

"How did you first learn to mine flint?" the boy asked. "And how did you find out that the best flint is the third layer down?"

A very old man answered. His body was bent with rheumatism (12). "When I was a boy I asked the same questions. My grandfather told me what his grandfather had told him. At first, long ago, men came here and found good flint on the surface. As time went on, they dug it all away. They noticed that it was a layer, not very thick, spread over the ground, and that it slanted downwards. So they dug down, following the flint, until they dared tunnel no further. Then they reasoned that if the layer was sloping down, they could go a little further off, and dig a great shaft till they reached the flint again. This they did, and found the flint, but they noticed that two layers of poorer flint had to be passed before the best was reached. It was such a great task to dig a shaft, that they learned to make tunnels along the flint to dig it away. These tunnels lead from the bottom of each shaft and from them much flint is brought up."

"The flint has not always revealed itself," said another man quietly. The other miners stirred uneasily.

"Once men dug a shaft, just like the others, but they found no flint," the man continued. "In the end, they had to leave it. But they did what they could to make their next attempt luckier. They took many lumps of fine flint, the best they could get from another shaft, and placed them in the bottom of the unlucky shaft. They arranged them in a triangle, pointing across the shaft to a flat ledge.

19

On this ledge they placed the statue of Mother Earth, carved in chalk. Then they filled in the shaft, and left it to the Earth, who had not seen fit to give them her gift of flint." This is the statue.

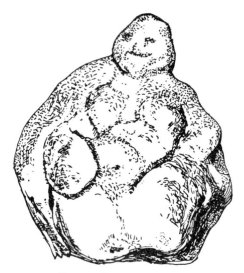

Statue of Mother Earth

Everyone was silent. Through the woods there came the howl of a wolf (8). The sun had set, and beasts were on the prowl. It was a long time before the boy could fall asleep. He had been excited to find the layer of the best flint, even though he had been expecting to find it. How much more excited must the first miners have felt when they dug the first deep shaft, only half believing they would find the flint. When their picks struck flint, they realized that their guess had been right after all!

Bonfire Night

It was summer-time when the traders brought the boy back to his own people. They followed the trackway along the top of the downs. At last the boy began to recognize landmarks and pointed out smoke from fires rising in thin columns through the trees.

"My father will be glad to see us," he said. "Now that he is in the summer camp, he will need flint for new axes. There will be much clearing to do for our new fields."

Presently the traders came to a gap in the trees. The ground was covered with grass and weeds. *Plantains* (13) grew everywhere. The trader pulled at one.

"We always know your people have been in places where this grows. It comes after you have grown corn on the land."

"These grow in our old fields, too." The boy pointed to red sprays of *willow herb* (13). "But this clearing will not be open for long. These little birch trees (13) will soon grow tall. Then it will be like the forest again, before we came."

"No," said the trader, thoughtfully. "Not just as it was. The tall trees do not grow as quickly as the birch. You cut them down, but they do not grow again. Your animals nibble the young shoots, so that where once there was forest there are now only bushes and undergrowth. You may think that this does not matter. But there may come a time when there are many more farmers wanting land. Now there is plenty. When your fields are exhausted you move away and cut down more forest. But what will happen when there is no more land?"

"There is always new land," said the boy.

"There will be new farmers. Perhaps one day your fields will be exhausted and you will move to new forest. Then, as you are cutting down the forest, another tribe of farmers will come and tell you that they came there first and that you must go away."

"I suppose we shall fight them with our bows and arrows."

"But if they beat you, you will have to go away. And if you have to go back to your old fields, you will not have so much food, as the soil will grow less and less corn. I have spoken about this to many farmers, when I traded with them."

The boy was not very worried about the future, however, for he had just spotted his own family. So he ran on ahead, his load of flint bumping on his back.

Soon the traders were on their way again and the boy told his father and mother all that he had seen and done. He even did some trading himself. He exchanged some of the fine black flint for a puppy, so that he would have his own dog to help him herding the cattle and sheep. The puppy would grow up to be a medium-sized dog, with long legs, looking rather like a collie (2).

This was the time of year when the farmers chose a place to make their cornfields. Large patches of *scrub*, with birches and hazel trees (13), showed where the old fields had been. Close by one of these, the farmers set to work to make a new clearing in the woods.

Men began to chip flint into axe-heads, or brought out their polished axes of flint or rock. The boy looked round for a branch to shape into a handle or *haft* for his own axe.

He used a flint scraper to strip the bark from the wood, then shaped his handle like the one in the picture. Fixing the handle to the axe-head was called hafting. His father had explained to him how the axe-head must fit tightly into the slot at top and bottom, but that the long sides of the axe must not touch the wood. The gap allowed the stone axe to vibrate when it struck the tree. The boy remembered the first axe he had hafted. He had fitted the stone head exactly into a slot, and was proud of the good fit all round. But when he showed it to his father, his father smiled and told him to try it out. So he struck a tree with his new axe and the axe broke. He never forgot that lesson! It took him a long time to make himself another polished flint axe.

A stone axe

When he had shaped the new haft, the boy went to his mother and asked for some leather. She found a soft strip for him and carefully he bound the axe-head in position.

In making the clearing, the very big trees were left alone, but the smaller ones were cut down and then the bushes and *saplings* were burnt. The farmers had found long ago that the ash from the burnt wood gave them an extra good crop of corn. They had tried growing corn on old clearings, but they never had such a good yield as in that first year when the ground was covered with a thick layer of ash (14).

The children enjoyed the burning of the woods as a change from the hard, dull work they did so often. Sometimes they burned themselves by mistake, but they ran in

23

and out of the smoke, black with ashes except for the whites of their eyes. They carried poles with which they raked unburnt branches on to places where the fire was burning fiercely. Where the undergrowth was thick, men rolled burning logs into it, until it caught fire.

When a shower of rain had cooled the ashes, and washed them into the earth, they brought out the corn that had been kept for seed.

"If we'd eaten this in the winter, when we were so hungry, we wouldn't have been able to sow it now," said the boy to his little brother.

The little boy seized a handful and scattered it on the ground. At once his elder sister sprang at him and smacked him.

"Pick it all up," she cried. "Each of these little seeds can grow into a tall plant which will make lots more seeds for us."

While the little boy crawled on the earth finding the corn, his sister laughed and said, "It's a pity we have to eat any corn this year; think what a lot we would have to sow next year then!"

The boy shrugged his shoulders. "It's the winter. There's always plenty to eat in the summer-time. We can hunt, and eat our own beasts too, and find apples (15) in the woods. But when the cold weather comes and we get really hungry, then we have to be careful not to eat too much corn. We can't kill our animals because we need them in the spring and the wild animals seem to be more difficult to hunt."

The boy went off to watch the farmers scattering the seed on the ground and then brushing the soil lightly over it with tree-branches. Some farmers sowed barley, but most of them sowed wheat (5). The boy knew that they would have to wait a few weeks before the green shoots sprang up. Before the second full moon from the time of sowing, the fields would be green.

In late summer, when the corn was golden-brown, the heavy heads were picked off, or cut with sharp flint blades. The husks were *threshed* away and the grain carefully stored.

When the corn was needed for food, the boy's mother would tell one of her daughters to make flour. The girl would kneel on the earth floor of the hut, in front of a heavy stone with a wide, smooth top which dipped in the middle, like a saucer. The girl laid a handful of corn in the centre of the stone and picked up a smaller, but heavy stone. She rubbed this round and round on the lower stone, gradually crushing the grains of corn into snow-white flour. She tried to be careful not to push the grains off the stone as she was crushing them, but some usually got spilt just the same.

After the harvest, it was time to meet their friends at the hill-camp, with all their animals. But the children were always sad to leave the clearing. They remembered the great burning, and how the fires glowed in the night, when the sparks flew up in the great clouds of smoke. That was the nicest work of all.

For many months the tribe had been planning to build their burial place. The tomb was to be a house for the dead, made of large stones set on end in the ground.

First the tribe had to decide where to build the tomb. They chose a hill, so that it could be seen from a long way off.

On the hill, people uprooted bushes, and cleared away the undergrowth. Down in the valley big grey stones called *sarsens* lay about on the grass. To drag these up the hill was a difficult task.

First, men cut down trees with flint axes, cut off the branches, and tied the tree-trunks together to make a platform. Then they levered up one end of a sarsen with big bars of wood, pushed the wooden platform underneath the stone, and levered up the other end of the stone, so that all the sarsen lay on the platform. Then they *lashed* the stone in position with ropes made of plaited leather thongs.

There were two ways of moving the stone on its platform. The platform could be used as a sledge and dragged along by men hauling on ropes. Or they could cut down more trees and lay the trunks down on the ground as rollers. The platform and sarsen would be levered up on top of the rollers. Then men would pull on long ropes, so that the platform and sarsen would move along on top of the rollers.

Fewer men were needed to pull the stone along when rollers were used. But many men had to move the rollers. Every time the platform was moved, the logs behind it had to be dragged up and laid on the ground in front of it. These men had to be quick. If it ran off the rollers, the platform had to be levered up on top of the logs again. Going uphill was very difficult. The pullers had to heave on the ropes all the time to stop the stone slipping backwards, while the rollers behind it were being carried round to the front.

At the place chosen for the tomb, a shallow ditch was marked out to show the plan. At the eastern end there was to be an entrance marked by a line of stones. In the middle of the line, a passage would lead into the tomb. From the passage, two pairs of small rooms would lead off to right and left. The passage would end in another little room. This is the plan of the tomb inside the long *barrow*. We

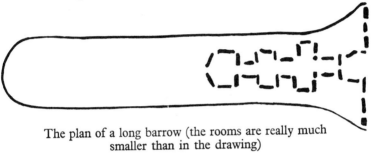

The plan of a long barrow (the rooms are really much smaller than in the drawing)

do not know why the barrow had to be three hundred and fifty feet long when the burial rooms were made right at the eastern end.

The walls of the rooms and of the passage were made with big sarsen stones set up on end in holes dug out with antler picks. It was impossible to make a continuous wall with the big uneven stones, so the spaces between them had to be filled in with other stones.

The tribe had noticed in their wanderings a lot of small flat stones in a place about ten miles away. So, while some people were moving the sarsens into position, others fetched these smaller stones, carrying them in packs on their shoulders.

The small flat stones were fitted between the sarsens to make a firm wall. The builders were clever. They had no cement to use to help the walls to stand up, but these walls have stood for about four thousand years.

Big flat sarsen stones were to be placed across the walls of the rooms and passage to make a roof. These stones were too heavy to be lifted by men, so they piled up earth and stones to make a slope to the top of the walls. Then the big stones were hauled up the slope on wooden rollers,

A wall inside a long barrow made without cement

and heaved across the walls. Gaps were filled in with the small, flat stones.

The roofs of the rooms and passage were to be covered over with a great mound of earth, or barrow, so that only the curving line of stones marking the entrance would be seen.

To get chalk for the barrow, a long ditch fifty feet wide was dug on each side of the tomb. As the chalk was levered out with antler picks, it was thrown up with shovels on to the mound of stones. At last all the stones were completely covered, and the surface of the mound was gleaming white chalk.

Now the tomb was finished. When anyone in the tribe died, the body would be laid to rest in one of the little rooms. With it would be placed a jar of food or drink, and some of the things that belonged to the dead man (16). After each burial, the entrance of the tomb would be blocked up, to keep strangers out. At last, when there was no more room for burials in this tomb, the entrance would be completely closed.

The tribe had noticed a particularly large sarsen; they thought their descendants would use this for the final barrier hundreds of years later. It would need about three hundred men to move it into position, for it weighed twenty tons (17). But it would keep people out of their family vault when the tomb was finally closed up.

When they had finished making the long barrow, the tribe looked at it proudly. For many years anyone who passed along the valley would look up and see it on the hill. Strangers would admire the skill of the people who had built it. Their tribe would be remembered as people who could move great stones and build with them, as well as breed cattle and grow corn to feed themselves. It would be a fitting last resting-place. This is what the tomb looks like today, now that the covering mould has been worn away.

The entrance to a long barrow

BRONZE AGE FARMERS AND TRADERS

The Family

THE village looked very peaceful on this warm summer day, three thousand five hundred years ago. Smoke from the fires inside the huts was rising lazily through a hole in the middle of each roof. Children with dogs were calling to one another as they watched herds of cattle and sheep grazing. From the woods lower down the hill came the sound of chopping as trees were felled to make a new hut.

A little girl was bending over the fire inside one of the round huts. She sat close to it, putting pebbles to heat in the reddest part. When she thought they were hot enough, she picked them up with a bent, green stick, and dropped them into a clay pot. The pot was full of stew. It was in a cooking-hole (18), dug in the ground beside the hearth and lined with flat stones. When the girl dropped a hot pebble into the pot, the stew hissed and sizzled. It would gradually become warm enough to eat. Smoke made her eyes water and she wished she could be out in the sunshine.

While the pebbles were getting hot, the little girl played with the baby. He crawled all over the earth floor of the hut and was very curious about the fire. The little girl longed for him to grow up so that she could make him fetch wood and water. She was always being told to go down to the river, or into the woods.

She was afraid of the woods because of the bears and wolves who lived there. Sometimes wolves came to the sheep pens and took lambs. It was horrible to hear them howling at night.

Her mother was grinding corn ready for the meal, like

Grinding corn

this. When she had finished, she felt the stew to see how hot it was. As it was not nearly ready, she sat down in the sun outside the hut to spin. A pile of stinging nettles lay there. The leaves had been stripped off and the stems were waiting to be beaten into *fibres*. Some fibre was already prepared and the mother took a mass of this in one hand. In her other hand she held a *spindle*. This was made of a piece of wood, about eight inches long, weighted

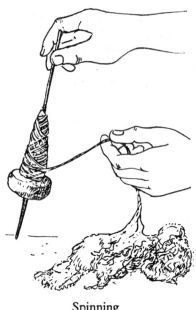

Spinning

with a small clay *spindle-whorl* (19). She drew out some fibres from the mass and tied them to the spindle. Then she twirled the spindle round and round, so that it made the fibres twist. Gradually the fibres became a fine thread. This was called *spinning*.

Now came the *weaving* of the thread into cloth. The thread was woven on a *loom* set up in one part of the hut. Two wooden posts were fixed in holes in the ground (20). Across the top was tied another post. *Warp* threads hung down from this post with a weight on the end of each thread, to keep it hanging straight down and to stop it becoming tangled with the others. The weights were either stones or lumps of clay.

Cloth was made by taking a thread in a *shuttle* in and out of the warp threads, under one and over the next. The children's mother was very pleased when one woman in the tribe showed her a way of saving time. She tied two rods across the warp threads. When one rod was lifted, it pulled forward every other thread, so that the shuttle could be passed across the cloth in one movement. Then the other rod was lifted. This picked out the threads in between those tied to the other rod. Then the shuttle was slipped back under these threads. It was a very quick way of weaving.

These *heddles* took a long time to prepare, although they saved time once weaving began. Sometimes by mistake two threads next to one another were tied to the same heddle. This meant that the shuttle was passed under two threads together, instead of alternate ones. Sometimes this mistake was not noticed until a wide strip of material had been woven. Then the weaver had to untie the heddles and tie the right threads to each one (21).

Thick, warm cloth was made from sheep's wool, which was coarse but could be spun and woven like the nettle linen (22). Linen and woollen cloth were made into clothes. The material was also used to wrap up tools and weapons which were buried with a man when he died.

A dead person was often wrapped in a long piece of cloth when he was laid to rest, under a round barrow of earth or stones.

While the children's mother was weaving, her eldest daughter was finishing a clay pot she was making. She was pricking a pattern all round the outside of her pot. Inside the pot she was drawing triangles with fine lines. She wanted to make the pattern fit exactly into the round pot and did not like hurrying over it. But her mother wanted her to scrape a skin—the skin of the calf whose meat had provided the stew. The fat had to be scraped off the inside of the skin, or it would become hard.

Her mother told the younger girl to leave the stew for a moment and find the skin-scraping tools for her sister. There was such a mess on the floor that it was difficult to see them. There were chips of flint, broken tools, bones from meals, pieces of broken cooking pots, and scraps of cloth lying about. At last she picked up a small flint scraper and a sharp flint knife-blade.

33

The elder girl sighed when she saw the flint knife. She had once seen a bright metal knife when traders had come to the village, and longed for one of these. Perhaps she would marry a man who could grow enough corn to exchange for one of these lovely new bronze tools

A flint and a bronze knife

This is the girl's flint knife and the bronze knife that the trader brought. Can you guess which is the flint knife? Why do you think the girl wanted a bronze knife?

Traders from Denmark

One day the little village was full of people. It was harvest-time. The barley from the small, square fields was being cut with sharp flint knife-blades. The heads were carried in baskets to threshing floors, where they were threshed to separate the seed from the *chaff*. Everyone was very busy. It was a good harvest.

A man came panting up the hill shouting that travellers were coming, with the warriors who always came to the village to get corn. They did not pay for it. They collected it in exchange for protecting the farmers from enemies.

34

The little girl was frightened of the warriors. They wore ornaments of gold and shining bronze, and had short, broad swords hanging from their belts. Important men among them carried a *sceptre* like this:

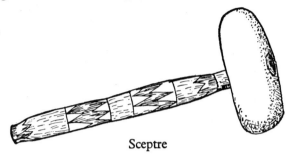

Sceptre

A long line of men climbed the hill, some with large packs on their backs. These were traders who had been across the seas exchanging metal objects made in Britain for things made in lands over the water.

The warriors and traders were given food and drink. As they ate, they argued among themselves. The traders wanted to pass through the warriors' lands to trade, and go across the Western Sea to Ireland. The warriors were always on the look-out for strangers who used the trackways across their lands. They made them pay for their protection. In this way they had got many fine objects from foreign lands, as well as those they bought from the traders.

The little girl crept up behind one of the warriors. He was wearing a necklace of bright blue stone beads (23). Here are some of the beads.

Beads

35

The warrior was looking down at a round, flat piece of yellow *amber* about as big as a man's thumb-nail in his hand. Round it was a wide, gold frame. The little girl thought it looked like the sun (24).

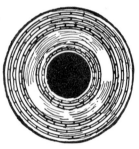

Pendant

The warrior looked up at the child and smiled. "Don't run away," he said kindly. The little girl saw that his shirt was fastened at the neck with round, black buttons (25). She sat down beside the warrior, who went on talking to the trader. In his belt was a dagger, in a wooden *sheath*. The hilt was made of wood, covered with patterns made by the heads of tiny gold pins hammered into the wood. It was pretty, and shone in the sunshine.

Dagger

36

Presently the warrior put something into her hand. "Here's something for you," he said. "It comes from across the sea. Take care of it."

This is what he gave the little girl:

Halberd pendant

It looked like a battle-axe, but was just over an inch long.

Another man looked at her present. "It is a *halberd*, like mine, but smaller," he said, holding up a dangerous-looking weapon. "In my land, over the sea in the direction of the sunset, we fight with these. It is a sharp, good weapon. I made it myself."

One of the little girl's brothers had come up to see what she was doing. "How did you make it?" he asked.

The man fumbled in his bag. "We use these lumps of *ore*. When we have worked on them, they change into shining bronze."

"I have never seen anyone making bronze," said the boy. "There are not many bronze tools in our village. Sometimes we trade with the warriors for one. But we have to give them much corn for a little bronze axe."

"So you have no-one living in your village making bronze?" The man spoke slowly, as if he were thinking.

"No. We are all farmers."

The man who could make bronze looked round at the village. He had learned his craft in Ireland, where he had been born. Then he had travelled eastwards across England with traders and settled in Denmark. There he had everything he wanted, but at last he decided to go home again, and so he had come across the sea with some Danish traders.

One of the Danes came through the crowd and knelt before the warrior. He took off his long cloak and spread it on the ground. Then he opened a little bag and a heap of amber spilled out on to the thick cloak.

The little girl thought that she had never seen anything so pretty as the smooth yellow stones. The warrior picked up pieces of amber and looked at them thoughtfully. In a few moments he was arguing with the man about what he would take in exchange. When they were his, he would have them made into a necklace.

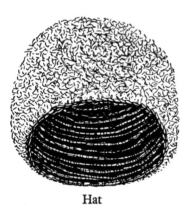

Hat

The trader took off his hat and laid it on the ground, for it was too hot to wear. The little girl put out her hand and felt the cap. It looked like fur (26), but the threads were strands of wool. They were sewn into the cap, which was made of several layers of woolly cloth sewn together, and had no brim.

The trader's tunic was made of wool. It was a wide piece of cloth wrapped round his body underneath his arms. Leather shoulder-straps held it up and a wide leather belt fastened the tunic round the waist. The trader's cloak was shaped like a capital **D**; one long side was straight, the other rounded. When the trader wore the cloak, the straight side was folded back a little to make a collar, as the cloak hung round his shoulders and fell well below his knees in deep folds. His shoes were made of an oblong piece of leather, gathered up at the toe and tied round the foot with leather thongs.

The foreign trader's wife had come with him. The little girl looked at her big but dainty ear-rings of thin gold wire. They were large enough for bracelets, the little girl thought. The woman's fair hair was kept tidy in a net made of horse-hair, and on top she wore a braided cap of wool, with long cords that hung down her back. She wore a woollen blouse, with elbow-length sleeves and button-hole stitch embroidery round the wide neck. This is what the trader and his wife looked like.

The traders from Denmark

39

The woman's skirt was very short, stopping a little above the knee, and it was made of strands of twisted woollen threads, woven into a band at waist and hem. It was cool to wear in warm weather. She wore a narrow belt, woven with a tassel at each end, and in front a big round bronze disc. This was new and very bright; it was decorated all over with patterns and had a sharp spike sticking up in the centre. The little girl thought that it must be uncomfortable to wear, especially when the woman had to bend down to pick up something (27).

At last the warrior and the trader agreed about the goods to be given in exchange for the amber beads. The warrior fetched some bronze axe-heads. The man who could make bronze picked one up. It was decorated with a pattern of fine lines across the blade.

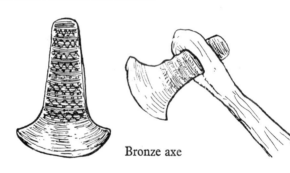

Bronze axe

"This comes from my country," he said, and laid it down again (28).

The little girl's brother felt the cutting edge of the axe.

"How quickly we could make a new hut if we had axes like this to cut down trees with," he said. "I would like to make axes like this."

"Perhaps you will, one day," the bronze-worker said, and smiled mysteriously.

The Bronze-maker or Smith

The bronze-maker had decided to settle in the village. In the eastern lands across the seas he had had many rivals. But he was the first smith to live in this village. Here he was able to get anything he asked in exchange for the bronze things he made, for the villagers did not want him to leave them and go to another village.

How he made bronze was kept a secret by the smith, but he had to have an assistant to help him. So one day he went to the little girl's father and suggested that his eldest son should become an apprentice. The boy was very proud indeed to have been chosen from all the boys in the village, but he found he had to work very hard.

One very hot day, in the next summer, the boy was crouching over the fire in the smith's round hut. Smoke was getting in his eyes, but he could not move away. He had to blow up the fire with a pair of bellows, to keep it glowing. The bellows were made of animal skin, with wooden handles. They had a clay nozzle to poke into the heart of the fire. The boy kept pushing the handles of the bellows up and down as fast as he could.

Propped up in the centre of the fire was a clay *crucible*. In it was tin and copper, which the smith was melting down into bronze.

The tin and copper had been separately melted down beforehand. The smith had exchanged goods with traders to get what looked like lumps of rock. These had been heated and had changed into shining metal cakes. The bronze-making stage was when the smith put a cake of tin in a crucible with nine times as much copper (29), and set the boy to melt it down in the fire.

Presently the smith came over and knelt down beside the boy. He jerked his head, and the boy put down the bellows and felt about for the green stick he had brought to the hut that morning. The clay crucible was so hot that the smith could not touch it with his hands. He used a green stick, because this could be bent round the crucible.

As the smith bent the stick, the boy moved towards what looked like a pile of flat stones. They were moulds, and looked like this:

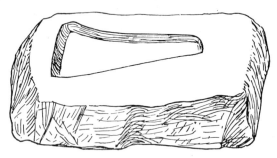

A stone mould for an axe head

The shape of an axe was hollowed out on one side of each stone. The boy blew the dirt out of them and laid several on the floor beside the smith, being careful to see that they were level. Then the smith lifted up the crucible. Very quickly, before the bronze could cool, he poured some into each mould except one. Then he turned to the boy, who eagerly took the crucible, heated it up again in the fire, and himself poured the metal into the last mould.

It was the first time that the boy had been allowed to pour out the valuable bronze, and he was very excited. The smith smiled as the boy put down the crucible.

"This is the first axe you have made," he said. "When it is cold, you can try your hand at sharpening it. If you make a good job of it, I will give it to you. You have watched me long enough. It is time you began to make tools yourself."

When the boy came to the hut next day, he went straight to the row of moulds. The bronze was now cold and the axes had a dull sheen in the sunshine. He picked up his mould and tipped out the axehead. It was heavy and he rubbed his hand over the smooth shiny surface. This is what it looked like.

An axe head made in a stone mould

"Don't let the fire out while you are admiring your work," called the smith. "Fetch some wood, and then you can help me sharpen the axes. Traders will soon come now that the corn is ripe and I must have a lot of tools ready for them to take away. I want to exchange them for a good supply of copper and tin from the West, for it may be a long time before we see them again."

The boy ran out of the village and quickly gathered some wood. He chopped up large branches with the stone axe his father had given him. Although the smith made bronze axes, not everyone in the village could afford to buy them.

"Now we'll see if you've used your eyes," said the smith when the boy came back with the wood. "How do I sharpen axes?"

The boy looked round for the smith's heavy hammer. Its head was made of a lump of rock, carefully shaped,

The boy beat the edge of his bronze axe with it. Under the blows the metal began to spread. At last the edge of the blade became thin and sharp.

"Don't beat it too long," warned the smith. "You don't want the edge to bend as soon as you start chopping."

The boy smiled. "I shall just hammer it flat again. I can't do that with the stone axes my father uses. Then he began to rub his axehead on a special flat rock made of sandstone to make it shiny.

While he was talking to the boy, the smith had been shaping wax into a model spearhead. The boy had found him the wax, from a nest of wild bees.

On the blade of the spearhead he drew a design of fine lines, with a sharp tool. Then he dipped the wax model into a pot containing *fine-grained*, very wet clay. This had plenty of water mixed with it, so that the clay could run into all the fine lines of the pattern. The smith took the model out and let some of the clay drip off.

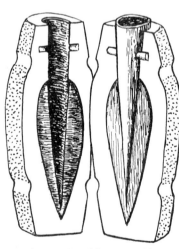

When a coating of clay had dried all over the spearhead, he encased it in coarse, stiff clay. Then he baked the clay with the wax model inside it. As the clay warmed and became hard, the wax model melted. He picked up the clay, and tipped the wax into a clay pot, so that he could use it again. There was now a hole, the exact shape of a spearhead, inside the clay mould. This was a mould for a

A spearhead in a mould

44

hollow spearhead. A crucible of bronze was heated on the fire again. The smith partly buried the clay mould in the ground to keep it upright. Then he poured in some *molten* bronze, but he did not fill the mould right up. To make the spearhead hollow, he pushed a long clay cone down into the mould. Then he saw that there was a thin circle of bronze all round the top of the cone, showing that there was enough molten metal in the mould.

When the metal had cooled, the smith broke the clay and took out the shining spearhead. It would fit over the end of a wooden shaft, and be fixed on with two bronze rivets and leather thong binding. There were deep grooves along the blade. Just below the blade, the smith had modelled two *bosses*.

The boy pointed to them and asked the smith what they were for. "They look like the heads of rivets," he said curiously.

"Once spearheads were made with rivets there," the smith told him. He drew with his finger on the earth floor. "The first spearheads of bronze were flat, made like the flat axes. Now we make hollow spearheads with rivet-holes at the side, not in the front. But our customers had become used to seeing them at the front, so there we make imitation rivets instead."

"But it means extra work," said the boy. "Couldn't I start making spearheads without them for you?"

But the smith did not seem too pleased by this suggestion. "You make what I tell you to make," he said.

The boy went to fetch wood for the fire. He knew that the smith made wonderful things, but he could not help thinking that it was foolish to make imitation rivets on a spearhead, for decoration. When he learned more, he would become a smith himself. He wondered whether it would be possible to make tiny bronze handles on each side of the spearhead, to help bind it into place. He sat down, drawing designs in the earth with a twig. The picture shows you what the smith and the boy drew.

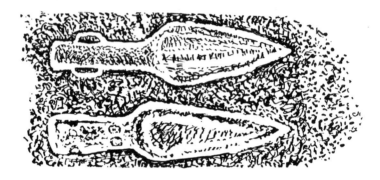

Spearheads

The Holy Place at Avebury

One day the little girl's father took the children to see the great holy place of their people. This was a great day, for they had only been to the temple at times of great ceremonies, when there had been so many people that they had hardly been able to see what the temple looked like.

The family walked down the hills and along the wide valley, until they saw ahead of them a great grassy wall. It curved away, in a great circle.

The children scrambled up the grassy bank after their father. At the top, they sat down and looked with awe at the sight below. This bank was always crowded with people at the festival time.

46

Below them was a deep, wide ditch. The inner side of the bank on which they sat sloped straight down into the ditch, which was a deep circle, cutting off spectators from the sacred ground inside. The little girl wondered whether she would be able to get out of the ditch if she rolled down the bank to the bottom. It looked a long way below.

On the wide grassy space inside the ditch, huge grey stones were arranged in a circle, standing just inside the edge of the ditch. They were wide and thick, and each was taller than a man. This is what they look like today (small markers mark the holes of the missing stones):

Avebury, Wiltshire

The ring of stones was broken at four places. Here entrances had been made. At each entrance there was a gap in the huge earth bank and there was no ditch.

47

The children asked how the big stones had been fixed in the ground.

Their father thought for a little while.

"I did not see this temple built," he said at last. "But if I were setting up a stone, I would do it like this. First I would have a deep hole dug in the ground. I would move the stone along to the edge of the hole, using tree-trunks as rollers underneath the stone. Then it would have to be tipped up on one end, and slid into the hole."

"You would have to be careful," said the bigger boy. "As the stone touched the ground, it would push a lot of earth from the edge of the hole right down to the bottom. You would have to make the hole extra deep to allow for that."

"A man told me what he had done once," replied his father. "They cut seven wooden stakes and arranged them in a curve in the ground at one side of the hole (30). The stakes took the weight of the stone as it slid off the rollers, so that it did not touch the edge of the hole at all. The stone slid down the stakes into the bottom of the hole."

The bigger boy thought about that. He decided to try

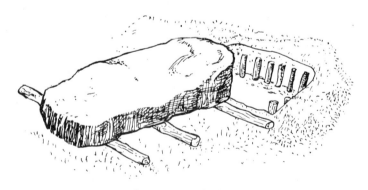

A stone near its hole

48

it with his friends when he went back to the village. There were plenty of big stones lying about on the downs. Of course, they would have to experiment with a little stone, to start with. He hoped that he would be able to work with really big stones one day.

"I would like to build a big temple, when I am a man," he announced.

His father smiled. "Perhaps you will build a new one here. You would not be the first to change the plan of this temple. Come with me."

The children followed their father along to the entrance on the south side. They climbed the bank again.

"Look into the great circle of stones," he said, "and tell me what you see."

"Two smaller circles of stones," the bigger boy said promptly. "And there is a group of stones in the centre of each."

"Long ago," said their father, "there was no huge outer circle of stones, nor any ditch or bank. There were three of these smaller circles, in a long line. A wide path led to the southernmost circle, which stood below us there. This was marked by pairs of great stones." (The two different shapes of stone that were used are shown in the picture.)

Stones marking the path at Avebury

49

"See those two huge stones? They marked the entrance into the smaller circle of our first temple (31). To this entrance led the wide path."

"Where is the wide path?" asked the little girl.

"There," said her younger brother, who had turned round. As they all looked, they could see two lines of stones, set on end, leading away in a curving path as far as they could see (32).

"Where do the stones lead?" asked the little girl.

"To the top of a hill," replied her father. "There is a little temple there; I saw it once. There are two circles of small stones there, one inside the other" (33).

The family ran down the bank again, and went across the grass to look at the stones marking the old path.

"This is a strange and wonderful place," said the older boy.

Stonehenge is Rebuilt

One day a band of warriors came to the village. They commanded that men should come with them to help with the rebuilding of their holy place.

Many families went with them, so that the women could cook for the men while they were working.

After a long journey walking southwards, over hills and through forests, they joined other bands of people going to work for the warriors. At last they came to a wide plain, with clusters of trees here and there. They noticed a wide path, marked by two lines of big stones, standing on end in the ground. The warriors followed this path, the sun shining on the gold-studded hilts of their daggers and on their short bronze swords.

The little girl was hiding something under her cloak. It was a bronze pin, as long as her hand. Its head was like a ball, and had a hole through it. She had picked it up near the remains of the fire when all the people were moving off after the night's stop.

The warrior who had given her the little battle-axe pendant walked by. She ran up to him and showed him what she had found.

"It's a cloak pin," he told her, and showed her how his cloak was fastened. He picked up a fold of cloth on each side of his neck, and pushed the pin through them. A short piece of thread was tied through the hole in the head of the pin. He wound the thread round the point of the pin, to stop it falling out, like this:

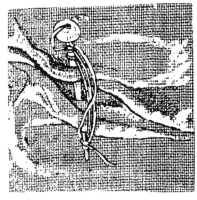

A pin tied in place on a cloak

The path marked by stones ended at the temple. This was surrounded by a deep ditch with an earth bank outside it where people watched the ceremonies inside the temple space. There was one entrance, marked by a gap in the ditch. A little to one side of the entrance stood a tall upright stone, with a ditch round it (34).

All round the enclosure, near the ditch, was a circle of holes, nearly filled in with earth. Inside this circle had been a double circle of blueish stones, each about four feet high. Only part of this double circle was still standing. As the new band of people came into the temple enclosure, they could see that most of the stones had been pulled down, leaving big empty holes in the ground (35). Many men were at work, tying ropes round the stones, and moving them with wooden levers.

One of the warriors seemed to be telling everyone what to do. He carried a sceptre like the one in the picture on page 35. He wore gold necklets and a gold bracelet. Small plates of gold decorated with patterns were sewn on to his clothes. Talking to him was another man, different from all the rest—a foreigner. He wore a short white tunic, and had a dagger stuck in his belt. He seemed to be giving the warriors advice about the temple.

Outside the ditch lay very large, long stones. There was a loud hammering sound as men battered them with stone *mauls*, to make their sides flat and smooth. The stones

Point on top of an upright stone at Stonehenge

were so hard that the men could not knock chips off them. Only a little grey powder was crushed away at each blow.

The little girl's brother managed to join the men who were working on these stones. It was hard work, but he soon learned how to hit the stones with the heavy maul the men gave him to use. He asked one of the other men what was going to be done with the stones. The man did not know. He thought that if the other stones were being pulled down, these stones would be put up instead. The man was not pleased to see the other stones being pulled down. It was not good to destroy an old temple. It had been standing as long as his people could remember.

The foreign man was giving directions to some of the stoneworkers (36). He said that the stones were going to be stood on end in the ground. Others were going to be put on top of them, as *lintels*, lying flat across the tops of the upright stones. He sent some men to cut down many trees. The trunks were needed to build a kind of scaffolding to raise the lintel to the level of the top of the upright stones.

Some of the men working on the stones discussed how to make the lintels rest on top of the uprights. They would have to be fixed so that they would not slip off.

Lintel stone with holes to fit over points on the upright stones

"If we were building in wood," said one elderly man, hammer in hand, "we should cut down the top of each upright at the sides until a point was left in the middle. We should cut a hollow in each lintel, to fit over the point on the upright. That could still be done in stone, though it would take longer to do than on wooden posts" (37).

"We should have to wait until the stones had settled in their holes," said another worker. "A stone is heavy, and takes some time to find its final position when it is stood on end in a hole. To make sure that the tops of all the stones were level, we should have to give them time to settle, and then cut the tops into points."

The lintel stones for the great circle had to be shaped very carefully indeed, like this, so that each one would fit into the stones on either side of it. You can see how

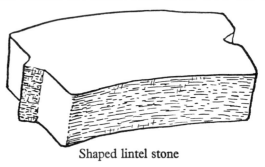

Shaped lintel stone

each stone was battered into a curve, so that the lintels themselves would form a circle. Each end of a stone was shaped so as to fit into the next. Can you see why this kind of joint is called "tongue and groove"?

It took a very long time to shape all the stones. Parties of men had to bring the great blocks of sarsen for the new temple from a place about twenty miles away. They arrived at the temple weary and dirty, after pulling the sarsens along on wooden sledges, moved with great levers. They used tree-trunks as rollers.

At last the warriors decided to begin erecting the stones. First they sent everyone outside the ditch. They had to mark exactly where to erect each stone. Once they were put up, it would be very difficult indeed to alter their positions.

The warrior chief first wanted to mark the exact centre of the temple space, enclosed by the ditch. Four small stones had been put up on end in the ground, just outside the bank. Ropes were tied round each pair of these stones, across the space. The centre was where one rope crossed the other.

Then these ropes were untied. A post was driven into the ground at the centre, with a long rope tied to it. One of the warriors picked up the end of the rope and walked away until it was stretched taut.

Then he began walking slowly round the post, keeping the rope stretched. Another man followed him, marking the ground where he had trodden. Soon the men came back to where they had started, having walked in a circle right round the post.

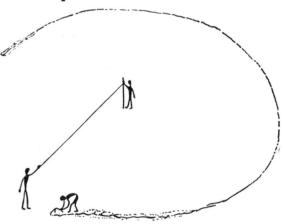

Marking out a circle

Men were now put to work to dig stone-holes all round this circle. This was to be the ring of tall stones with lintels lying across their tops.

Inside this circle the biggest stones of all were to be erected. They had to be dragged inside before all the stones of the outer circle were put in their holes.

Five pairs of holes were dug for them, forming a horse-shoe. The biggest pair of stones was set up in the centre of the horse-shoe, and the two shorter pairs at the ends. After the stones had settled in their holes, the tops were shaped. Then a lintel was hoisted on top of each pair (37). In front of the largest pair of stones, two stones were set up on end. They were made of sandstone, and were different from the grey sarsens (38). These stones were placed so that the first rays of the sun on the morning of midsummer day would fall between them (39).

When all this work was done, the people could see that the warriors were arguing among themselves. The trouble seemed to be about what was to be done with the stones from the old temple.

In the end, men were told to dig two circles of holes outside the great sarsen circle. It was very difficult to dig these holes in perfect circles, for a man could no longer walk round holding a rope from a post in the centre of the temple because the big stones that had been put up were in the way. These circles should have been marked out with the rest.

When the holes were all dug, the warriors had another argument and decided not to put stones in them after all! (40). Instead, men were told to dig holes, not outside, but inside the great sarsen circle! The bluestones from the old temple were put up on end in these holes, in a circle between the great sarsen circle and the sarsen horse-shoe. The biggest stones from the old temple had been sorted out. They were put up in a horse-shoe inside the sarsen horse-shoe.

When it was all finished, there were many stones crowded into a small space, but the temple was very impressive. Some of the people were very pleased to see the stones from the old temple being used in the new one after all. Here you can see Stonehenge as it is today, and what it looked like when it was built.

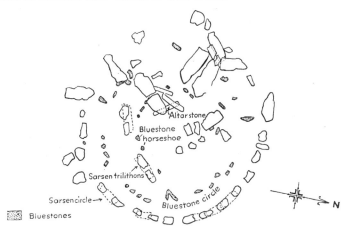

Plan of Stonehenge in 1957

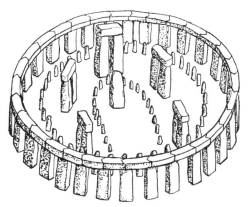

Stonehenge as it was in the Bronze Age

As the families were getting ready to go back to their villages, the boy heard the sound of hammering. He saw the foreign man standing by one of the big sarsens in the horse-shoe of tall stones, battering it with a hammer-stone. The boy went up to see what he was doing. He saw that axe-heads had been carved on the flat surface of the stone. But the foreign man was not making an axe-head.

Dagger and axe carvings

Suddenly the boy realized what the carving would be. As the man's arms were lifted, the boy saw the dagger in his belt. The top of the blade was shaped into two points, which stuck out on either side. It was different from the daggers worn by the warriors (41).

The man smiled as he saw the boy watching him.

"Men will see my work and know that a stranger worked here," he said. "I will leave this behind me before I return to the south. Perhaps one day you will be a trader. Come to my country with the yellow stones from the north (42). In my land you will see many fine buildings in stone. Then you will come back and build an even better temple than this—who knows?"

IRON AGE CELTS

A Comfortable Home

(Fourteen hundred years have passed since the boy watched Stonehenge being rebuilt)

A MAN stood outside the door of his farmhouse. It was very early and the sun had just risen. He wanted to think of all the jobs that had to be done.

He made a list in his mind of things to do. The grain pit should be opened today and the seed corn put into baskets ready for sowing. His wife and the other women could do that. The plough should be taken to the fields by one of his brothers, while another could fetch the oxen from their stalls. Their wives and children could keep the birds off while the seed was being scattered. His old mother would sit at the farmyard gate when they had all gone and stop intruders coming in. If the gate were left open, thieves might take the corn and tools, or a wolf might slip in silently to carry off a lamb.

The noise of the family getting up came through the doorway. The man picked up a bronze bucket, with wavy sides. He took the wooden cover off a pit full of water, dipped the bucket in, and took it over to the sheep and cattle. Here is his bucket:

Bucket

59

Pot made by a farmer's wife

Girls and women came with buckets and milked the cows. The farmer's wife made porridge for breakfast in a big clay pot. The fire was in the middle of the house. Above it there was a hole in the roof where the smoke could escape. The farmhouse seemed full of grown-ups and children, for one big family lived in the house. There were the man, his wife and children, and his old parents. Then there were his brothers, their wives and children, and his sisters who were not married. Two of his sisters were married, and had gone to live with their husbands' families.

As the family was so large, a very big farmhouse had been built (43). It was round, fifty feet across, and built on a stout wooden framework.

The wooden framework of a farmhouse

60

A farmhouse

This is what the house looked like when it was finished. The outside wall was made of tree-trunks split down the middle, placed side by side in a trench. Inside this wall, with a wide space between, was another circle of wooden posts to hold up the roof. Hurdles and curtains had been put up to divide this space into little rooms.

It was dark and smoky inside the house, even in the day-time, although some light came through the smoke-hole. The fireplace was in the middle and everyone gathered round it to have their meals and listen to stories when the day's work was done. The children liked the stories. Some of them were about the gods of their people, like Lug the sun-god and Manannan the sea-god (44). Others were about the deeds of their ancestors who lived long ago. Sometimes a travelling story-teller came to the farm. Then the family had a feast and heard new stories.

From outside, the walls of the house could not be seen. They were covered by the roof, which came right down to the ground all round, except over the doorway. There it was held up by two rows of wooden posts to form a porch. The roof was made of turf, and kept out the rain very well.

All round the farmyard was a high wall or *palisade* of split tree-trunks. As the man went towards the farmhouse for his breakfast, he remembered that he must look all round the palisade to mark all the rotten timbers, for he had woken up in the night to hear the howling of wolves. He would trust no-one to do this but himself.

After breakfast he set all the family to work. Children with dogs drove sheep and cattle out to pasture. Ploughing began in the fields near the farm where land had been cleared of trees. The farmers cultivated about thirty acres, which was divided into two parts, for corn was sown twice every year. In the autumn, wheat was sown. This was a strong plant and could grow through the long wet winter. In the spring the weaker barley was sown, which needed warmer weather for growing.

The farmers knew that they had to keep the soil in good heart if they were to keep growing crops on the same fields. They found that it was good for the fields if they dug chalk from the ground and spread it over the surface. They also manured the ground by letting cattle graze after the corn had been cut. So they were able to grow crops in the same land year after year. This meant that they did not have to keep moving house to make new clearings in the woods.

The soil was good and fertile, and the farmers reaped about five *bushels* of corn from every acre that they sowed. This gave them plenty of corn for their own needs. Although they killed off many of their beasts in the autumn, they were able to feed a good number through the winter on corn, provided they had a good harvest.

Presently the man was watching his brothers *yoke* the two oxen to the wooden plough. The wooden yoke was laid across the necks of the patient animals and leather thongs fastened yoke and plough together. The plough was a very simple one. It did not cut the soil deeply and turn the top soil underneath, for it had no *mouldboard* or *coulter*. The *ploughshare*, which broke up the earth, was a pointed wooden stake, made extra hard by being burnt in the fire. The fields were ploughed first from one side, then from the next, so that the furrows crossed one another at right-angles.

The farmer watched the flocks of birds circling behind the ploughman. He would have to pray to the gods to make the seed grow, he thought.

The Harvest

Red-gold corn was waving in ripples under a stormy sky. The farmer decided to begin bringing in the harvest, although a light rain was falling. He knew that he would be very lucky to have enough sunny days to dry out the corn, even though it was high summer (45).

Everybody in the family helped in the fields at harvest-time. There were no *scythes*. Corn was cut with a curved iron sickle on a wooden handle, like this one:

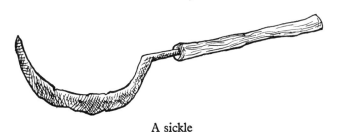

A sickle

Meanwhile, women were making big clay ovens in the farmyard to dry the grain. Small children were sent down to the stream to get clay. They enjoyed doing this as it was an excuse to play in the water, until one of their mothers came to see what they were doing, with a stick in her hand.

The man's eldest daughter was making an oven. It was a dome of clay, with a hole where the grain would be put in to dry out over the ashes of the fire. Her two cousins kept telling her to hurry up, as they were waiting to light the fire in her oven. She told them they would have to wait until the clay had dried out.

An oven for drying corn

When the oven was ready, the boys lit a fire in it. They used two fire-stones which they had found with glittering iron *pyrites* in them. When these were knocked together, a spark flew out and kindled the dry leaves and *fungus*. "Hurry up," said the girl. "I could light a fire quicker than that with two sticks!"

64

When the fire was glowing, the girl fetched a big basket of damp heads of corn. She scattered the corn in the oven and told the boys to watch and see that it did not burn. The boys crouched by the oven, which was pleasantly warm. They watched everyone running about the farmyard, raking in ovens, fetching water, and shouting at animals and children. From inside the farmhouse came the sound of a *quern* grinding corn.

The boys sighed. It was boring sitting by the oven, but at least it was not hard work. "Shall we play dice?" one of them suggested. He hurried into the farmhouse, being careful to avoid his father in case he was given a job to do. When he came back, he threw the flat bone dice on the ground. The boys scooped them up in turn and shook them in a bone cup.

Presently they looked up to see the man standing over them. His daughter came hurrying up. "We've been working together," she said. "I made the oven and the boys have been watching the corn while I ground some corn for mother." She opened up the oven and raked out some blackened grains. "It's burnt!" she cried in dismay.

Her father's face darkened, and he gripped his staff. Even though the harvest was good, it was serious to lose corn in this way. "I'll see that you remember this day's work of yours," he said. "You'll eat no corn of mine tonight, and you'll spend it in the yard!"

He caught sight of the boys' father, and shouted to tell him what had happened. A crowd gathered round the smoking oven. The boys were beaten.

Inside the farmhouse the girl was quickly mixing flour into a stiff paste with water. She was alone by the hearth as all the women had gone to watch the beating.

When the flour was mixed, the girl made it into round balls, which she flattened between her hands. Then she raked a hole in the warm embers and pushed the buns in (46). She marked the places with pieces of broken pot, so that she would know where to find the buns. She could slip them to the boys when the family was settling down for the night. If they had no supper, they would be very hungry.

Next morning, the two boys had disappeared. Their mother cried. Their father tried to track them with dogs, but the hounds lost the scent at the stream. Only the girl knew what had happened to them. When she had slipped out of the farmhouse in the dark with the hard buns, she had found the boys tying up their possessions in a piece of cloth. They had told her that they were going to run away to join the traders. They wanted to ride in *chariots* all over the land, not spend all their lives at the farm where they had been born. The girl was sorry, as she would be lonely without her cousins. She wished that she could run away too.

After the excitement about the boys' disappearance had died down, people set to work again.

The corn that had dried out in the ovens was threshed. It was tipped in buckets on to a flat space in the farmyard. Then it was beaten with *flails* until the coarse husks were loosened, showing the golden grains of corn that had been hidden inside them.

After corn had been threshed, it was *winnowed*. Women and children picked it up in small baskets and tossed it high into the air. The loosened husks were blown away on the wind, and the heavy grain fell to the ground. The children enjoyed the winnowing. It was the only time of year when they were allowed to play with the precious corn. Corn that had been winnowed was collected and stored in deep pits, lined with matting.

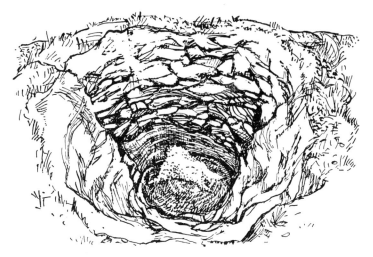

A deep pit for storing corn

In spite of the threshing and winnowing, a good many husks remained with the corn. Also, the seeds of weeds, like wild oats, were mixed up with the corn. No-one bothered to sort them out (47).

The kind of wheat that these farmers grew had very tough husks. That was why they had to dry it out in the clay ovens before they could thresh it. This was a risk to the harvest, for if many careless people let the corn burn, as the two boys had done, a good harvest could be wasted. Often the corn was slightly burnt by being heated too long (48). But it was put into the corn pits, in case even this might be needed before the long winter was over.

The harvest had been safely gathered in, and the farmers were planning which of their animals they would keep through the winter.

Suddenly there was shouting at the gate in the palisade. It was a man from a farmhouse not far away. He came with a warning. The people of the valley towards the sunset were gathering for war. All the farmers of their own valley were planning to move up into the hills to defend their property. He told the man which hill had been chosen for their retreat. They were going to make a big fort as soon as they could get there.

When the messenger had gone, the man sent one of his brothers to warn the family at the farmhouses where his married sisters lived. Then he began to plan.

Cattle and sheep were rounded up. Corn was put into baskets, and slung on the backs of the women and older children, with other precious possessions. Then the whole family set off, feeling sad at leaving their comfortable home.

At last they saw the hills rising before them. They walked up a long slope, covered with trees, until they reached the top. On all sides, except the one they had walked up, the hill sloped down very steeply to the valley below. The steepness of the hill would help to protect them from their enemies.

Some families had already arrived and had started work. The head men of the families were working out the plan of the fort.

First a plough was driven round the top of the hill, to make a furrow to guide the people who were to dig the ditch. The loosened chalk and soil were used to make the *rampart* above the ditch.

The rampart was built up between two walls of solid chalk blocks which were supported by a framework of timber. Then the space between the walls was filled up with the rubble from the ditch. Men stood on the rampart to de-

Marks of the wooden posts of the rampart found at a hill fort

fend the fort. When they were fighting they were protected by a wooden fence, along the outside edge of the rampart. This is what the rampart looked like before the fence or palisade was built along the top of it. The picture at the top of the page shows the marks left in the earth from which the archaeologists work out how ramparts were made.

Making the rampart of a hill fort

69

There were two gates into the hill-fort. These had to be strongly guarded. It would be very difficult for an enemy to get into the fort by crossing the ditch and climbing the high rampart. It was more likely they would try to storm the gates. These were made of wood, and were very heavy.

After many days' hard work, the fort was finished. Cattle and sheep were allowed to graze outside in the daytime but at night they were driven inside into pens. The people put up small huts inside the hill-fort and dug pits to store the corn they had brought with them.

Then one day they saw a great column of smoke climbing up into the still autumn air. It came from a burning farmhouse. Soon they saw more smoke, as another home was looted and burned. The men sharpened their spears and waited for the battle.

A few days later they heard their enemies coming up the hillside, shouting as they came. They were driving with them cattle they had captured from families who had not been warned that they were coming. They had captives, too, bound with ropes, who might be sacrificed to the gods, or made to work as slaves.

The enemy sent scouts round the hill-fort to see if they could find a weak place in the defences. The men on the ramparts hurled spears at them if they came within range, but mostly they kept out of reach, and shouted insults at the men in the fort.

The leader made a long speech to his men, telling them to be bold and victory would be theirs. There was much shouting and waving of spears.

Then the people inside the hill-fort saw a band of men coming to attack one gateway. The defenders climbed the rampart and stood on the wooden platform on top. They were protected by the wooden fence, as they hurled

70

spears and stones at the enemy. Suddenly above the noise of the battle there came shouts and screams from the other end of the hill-fort. The attack on one gateway had been only a pretence. The main attack was just being made on the other entrance, and the few men left there had been taken by surprise.

A boy was sent running as fast as he could to the first battle, to tell the men there to come to the other entrance, where there was a big crowd of attackers trying to set the gates on fire.

The defenders were in serious trouble. There were not enough men to fight in two places at once. Suddenly, to their surprise, the attackers drew back from the first gateway. There was shouting from the hillside, and a jingling of harness. Horses neighed and the sun came out to shine on the glittering bronze fittings of chariots.

"It's the traders!" said the men inside the hill-fort. They wondered whose side the traders would take in the fight. Then, to their relief, they saw men getting out of the chariots, and rushing towards the enemy with drawn swords. Some chariots were driven round to the other gateway, where the soldiers in them jumped out and began to fight, while the charioteers held the horses at a safe distance.

The men in the hill-fort opened one of the gates and rushed out to join in the battle. Their enemies were now outnumbered, and were soon put to flight, leaving behind them the cattle and prisoners.

Soon all the men were talking together and the farmers thanked the traders for coming to the rescue. The girl saw her father ordering baskets to be filled with corn as a gift to the traders. She looked for a bronze bucket and, filling it with water for the horses, walked out of the fort

71

to where the chariots had been left. Boys were standing by the heads of the horses. Two of them turned round as the girl came towards them. She stared at them. They were her cousins, who had run away from the farm!

"Look out, you're spilling the water," one of them called. "Did you see us behind the chief's chariot"?

They told her how they had met the band of traders soon after running away. The traders had allowed them to join the band as horse-boys. One day they would be charioteers and drive chariots for the warriors.

The girl's father asked the traders how they had come to the hill-fort. They told him that two boys had joined them. The boys had been worried by the smoke of burning farms and had asked them to find their family. They had promised that the family would buy many things from them, if they would go to trade with them. So they had gone to the farm, but they had found nobody there. Then they had met a family who told the traders where people were going to make a hill-fort. The traders liked the boys. They were strong and willing, and worked well. So they agreed to go to the hill-fort, to see if their family was safe.

Now that the enemy had been defeated, the farmers would be able to go back to their homes. But first they gave the corn they had brought with them to the traders. Some of it was a gift, because the traders had helped them. Some of it they exchanged for the iron tools and bronze brooches that the traders carried on their pack-horses.

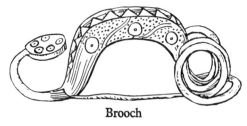

Brooch

72

That evening there was to be a feast. Calves were killed and cut up into joints of meat. The traders' wives showed the farmers' wives the big bronze *cauldron* in which they cooked their meat. It was made of strips of bronze riveted together. It was very old, and patches had been fixed over holes in the bottom. The women explained that cauldrons were difficult to make and expensive to buy. They had to make one last a long time.

Cauldron

There were two heavy rings at opposite sides of the rim These were hooked on to chains, and the cauldron was hung on an iron frame over the fire. Water was put in and then the joints of meat. A little girl was told to stir the stew with a stick.

Then the wife of the leader of the traders brought out a bundle wrapped in a cloth. She opened the cloth, and showed the farmers' wives a block of white salt (49). She broke off a piece and threw it into the stew.

When the stew was cooked, the men left their work and gathered round the fire. The sun was going down. Horses had been tethered safely inside the gates of the fort. Sentries were on guard by the gates, in case of any surprise attack.

The traders showed the farmers their custom at a feast. By the cauldron lay a two-foot-long fork, with two prongs.

Fork

73

Each man in turn came up to the cauldron and stabbed the fork into it. Whatever he brought out on the fork he ate for his supper. If he missed, and brought out nothing, everyone laughed at him.

After they had eaten, the men called on a story-teller who was travelling with the traders to tell them a tale. He told them about a strange pig (50).

"You all know that the image of the pig is placed on shields by men who work in metal, so that he will help warriors in battle. He himself is a desperate fighter when

Model pig from a helmet crest

hunted by men with dogs, and warriors bear his image with them that his courage may be theirs when they attack their enemies." This pig was worn as a helmet crest. On page 75 is a shield which was decorated with a pig design.

Everyone was quiet, leaning forwards as they crouched round the fire on the grass. Children crept up to listen, and stroked the dogs as they lay behind their masters.

The story-teller went on with his tale. Once there was a chieftain who owned a huge and famous pig. There were two kings who each longed to possess the pig because each thought it would make him the most important king in the land.

So both kings sent a group of men to ask if he could buy the pig. The owner of the pig was very worried indeed. He knew that the king who did not get the pig would take revenge on him. He was so worried that he made himself ill. At last his wife asked him what was the matter. When he told her, she said, "Tell each chief that he can have the pig. Then, when they come for it, they can fight it out for themselves."

This seemed the only thing to do. But when the day for handing over the pig arrived, so many people came with the two kings to fetch the pig that the pig itself had to be killed to provide meat for the feast. So neither king could take it away with him. But the trouble did not end there. Each king thought that he should have the best joint of pork.

So they called on their best warriors, one by one, to fight a duel to decide which king was to have the best joint. But every time a warrior stood up to fight, a man on

Shield decorated with a pig

the other side would make him look ridiculous, by reminding him that he had once run away from a fight, or telling him about some other time when he had not distinguished himself as a brave fighter.

In the end the kings and their men became so angry that there was a great battle in the house of the owner of the pig, and many men were killed.

One of the kings was on his way home in his chariot when he had an unpleasant surprise. A warrior had been hiding underneath the chariot as it drove along. He climbed up into the back of the chariot and suddenly caught the king from behind. In exchange for his life, the king offered the warrior all that he had. The warrior said that he would like to live at the king's house for a year, with everything that he wanted provided. And there was nothing for it but for the king to agree.

That was the end of the tale. The sky was dark, and

75

stars were shining. The face of the story-teller was lit by the firelight.

All the men listening knew that the king could not have harmed the warrior while he was living at his court. His promise was sacred, and it was better for a man to die than break a promise.

*   *   *   *

Next day the two boys who had joined the traders were standing on the ramparts of the fort.

They saw a band of people coming up the hill towards the fort. They were not enemies, for they did not seem to be armed. Among them were women and children, and pack-horses with large bundles tied on each side of their backs.

In the middle of the band was a straight line of more people, one behind the other, very close together. The boys wondered how they kept the same distance apart all the time. As the strangers came nearer, the boys heard the clanking of chains. Then they saw that a long chain joined the line of people together. Someone stumbled and fell down. As he fell, he pulled other prisoners down on top of him. A man came and hit them all with a stick until they managed to stand up again.

The boys ran to the gateway of the hill-fort, and watched the line of prisoners pass inside. They looked tired and their necks were red and sore where the iron hoops rubbed them. You can guess from the picture how painful it must have been to wear them. The one who had fallen down looked at them enviously as he stumbled by: he was little older than the boys.

76

Slave chain

That evening the boys listened carefully as the strangers told their hosts about their journey. They belonged to a people called Belgae. They lived across the sea in what is now called Belgium (51). They were travelling to the island called Mona (Anglesey), where they had heard that Druids lived, with their sacred groves of oak-trees. British Druids were famous even where the Belgae lived, because of their learning, and knowledge of the laws. But great as their knowledge was, they held terrible ceremonies, when they sacrificed human beings to the gods.

The king of one tribe of Belgae was sending men to the Druids, with rich gifts and captives, because he wanted the help of the Druids in deciding some problem that troubled him. The Druids would accept the gifts, sacrifice the captives, and give the Belgian visitors a message for their king.

The farmer's daughter came up quietly behind her cousins. "How did they choose the captives?" she whispered.

"They were probably prisoners caught after a fight," said one of the boys. "It might have happened to you if we hadn't brought the traders to find you."

"I know," she said. "I only wish that boy wasn't going to be sacrificed. He looks very ill. I'm sure he will die if he has to walk much further. Father says that Mona is many weeks' journey from here."

A plan was forming in the boys' minds. They told the girl to stay near the fire, and warn them if any of the Belgae went over to look at the captives. If she knocked two stones together, they would lie down and hope that they would not be seen in the darkness. They walked quietly over to where the prisoners were asleep. In the faint moonlight they made out the figure of the boy. One of the cousins put his hand over the boy's mouth, in case he made a noise when he woke up. The other boy touched his cousin's arm. He had heard a jingling of metal as a guard moved. He pushed the boy down, and, wandering over to the guard, began to talk to him about his own country. The guard was soon telling him about the fight in which the captives had been taken prisoner.

Meanwhile the other cousin was running his hand round the iron ring. He found that he could not possibly undo it.

The slave woke up. He felt very hot and feverish. As he stirred, he moved the chain. The cousin's hand slipped on to one link of the chain, where it joined the neck-ring. Even in the darkness he could tell that it was old and worn. In one place the thick link had been worn thin. The boy tried to twist it in his strong fingers. He slipped a dagger out of his belt, and bent the iron against it. At last he felt it break. He slipped the neck-ring off the link, and slowly drew the slave out of the ring, keeping the chain as still as possible so that the links would not jingle and make the guard suspicious.

He clasped the slave's hands round one of his own ankles, and crawled away. He led him like this round the edge of several pits, and then, when they had passed round a hut, he sat up.

The slave-boy was free!

Next day the Belgae made a great commotion. They had discovered the escape of the boy and were hunting for him everywhere. The cousins and the girl were listening to the talk as much as they could, to find out what plans were being made to recapture the boy. They were dismayed when they heard the girl's father offering the Belgae his own dogs to track down the boy.

"The dogs will find him at once," said one of the cousins. "Not if they take them outside the gates before they let them loose," replied the girl. "They are sure to think that he climbed the ramparts and ran off into the woods."

"Well, if they start looking inside the fort, the dogs will go straight to the grain pit where we left him."

"They won't think of looking there, unless they do let the dogs loose inside the fort," said the girl. "I still think it was a good place to hide him."

In the end they decided to tell the girl's father. At first he insisted that they should give up the boy. It was a serious matter to take a slave from the gods. Their anger might fall upon him and make the crops fail next year. The boys pointed out that the prisoner was ill, and that they had often been told that only the best was good enough for the gods.

The man thought for a few minutes. Then he said, "We will buy the boy from the Belgae. I will do this for you, as you saved our people from being made slaves themselves."

He told them to come with him. He led them to the place where he had buried his wealth. He had no coins to buy things with. His people had once given swords in exchange for food and iron tools. Now they used long bars of iron. These looked like partly-made swords. They were made by smiths in different lengths, each with its own value. This is an iron currency bar. We do not know what value each one had.

Iron currency bar

The man dug away the earth, and pulled some bars out of the pit. Then he filled up the hole, and put back the turf, looking round to see whether anyone had noticed what he was doing. He did not want anyone to see where his wealth was buried, so he always had to be careful when he went to dig it up. It would have been easy for a thief to steal some. Where do people keep their wealth nowadays?

The chief man of the Belgae argued for a long time with the farmer. But in the end he agreed that the boy might not have been good enough to sacrifice to the gods. He had become ill when crossing the sea and had not recovered.

The Belgae took the iron bars from the farmer in exchange for the boy and loaded them on one of the horses. Then they set off on their long journey to the north-west. The other slaves went with them.

The traders were very pleased with the trade that they had done with the farmers. They had obtained many things that they needed. They were especially pleased to have exchanged iron tools for some tin. They never had enough bronze, and they needed tin to make it with.

The leader of the traders decided to have a new chariot made. The two boys were sent out to cut down trees to cut into planks to make the floor of the chariot. It was to be four feet square. Iron saws and *adzes* in wooden handles were used to shape the wood.

A thick axle was made, and fixed under the floor, to attach the two wheels to the chariot. The *wheelwright* shaped the wheels. Each was about three feet across. It had nine spokes, which were fixed into the rim or 'felloe'. The felloe was one long piece of wood, bent into a circle. The ends were held together with iron clamps.

Two semi-circular screens of hurdle were woven. These were to form the side walls of the chariot. It had to be open at front and back. In front, the charioteer had to be able to move freely to control the two ponies. The back was left open to allow the warrior to jump in and out. He did not fight from the chariot. He was driven up to a battle. Then he left the chariot, and sprang into it either to retreat or to chase a beaten enemy.

While the carpenters were at work, the blacksmith was preparing iron to make metal fittings for the chariot. First he took lumps of iron-ore from his pack. He had picked these up as the traders passed by a place where there was plenty lying about on the surface of the ground. Iron-ore was not difficult to get, like tin or copper. But people had only been able to use it when they invented a kind of small furnace that could make ore very hot. Iron could not be *smelted* at such a low temperature as copper.

The blacksmith and his young assistant made the furnace of pieces of stone and clay. When the ore melted, the pure iron formed lumps or 'blooms', and the other minerals that had been mixed with the iron melted into 'slag', which was thrown away.

The smith opened up the furnace, and took out the pure iron, in long iron tongs. Then he heated this again in a fire. When it was red-hot, his assistant held it in the tongs over an anvil, while the blacksmith beat it with a heavy stone hammer into the shape he wanted.

Blacksmiths could not cast iron in moulds, as they could cast bronze. They could not make a furnace hot enough to make iron melt. To shape things of iron, the assistant had to keep heating the iron, and the blacksmith had to hammer it while it was red-hot.

For the chariot, the blacksmith beat out iron tyres for the wheels. These were strips one and a half inches wide, and one-fifth of an inch thick. When they were finished, the wheelwright 'sweated' the tyres on to the wooden felloe of the wheel. The tyres were heated until they were red-hot, then placed round the wheel. When they cooled, they contracted and became slightly smaller, gripping the wheel tightly.

The hub of the wheel was covered with a metal band. This looked pretty, and shone in the sun, if it were made of bronze. But as bronze was expensive and iron was cheap, the blacksmith made a band of iron, then coated it with thin bronze. It was not only an ornament. It protected the hub from wear, and stopped it splitting.

A wheel was fixed on each end of the axle. The end of the axle passed through the centre of each wheel. To keep the wheel on, an iron *linch-pin* was pushed through a hole bored through the end of the axle.

When all parts of the chariot had been put together, it was ready except for the horses. The leader of the traders bargained for these with one of the men in his band. He exchanged a fine gold necklet and some other precious things for a pair of small ponies.

They were brought up to the front of the chariot (52). An iron bit, coated with expensive bronze, was placed in the mouth of each pony. Leather reins were fastened to the bits. These passed through a ring or 'terret' fixed on top of the yoke, and then were held by the charioteer. The picture shows a terret and horse's bit.

Horse's bit and terret (right)

A yoke four feet long had been carved from a stout tree-trunk. It was curved to fit over the necks of the ponies. From the yoke, a leather strap passed round the throat. As the pony moved forwards, it dragged the chariot after it. But the pressure on its throat stopped it from moving as fast as it could have done if a horse-collar had been used.

The first people to harness the horse thought that it could be treated like the ox. Oxen had been harnessed under a yoke for many hundreds of years. But a horse's body is different from that of an ox. People did not make the best use of horses until the horse-collar was invented, many centuries later.

Gay blankets had been laid across the backs of the ponies. The chariot looked very beautiful with coloured blankets and shining bronze fittings. The traders' leader and his charioteer climbed in. The two boys let go the bridles. It was time to move on. The boys said goodbye to their family, and ran down the hill after the traders, with their chariots and pack-horses.

The girl watched them for a long time, feeling very sad. She wondered whether she would ever see them again. There had been talk of much fighting going on. Still, she had a new companion—the slave-boy they had rescued from the Belgae. He was going to live with them on the farm, as he would be useful now that the two boys had gone. He had never liked fighting and wanted to settle down as a farmer.

The farmers were packing their goods again. They were going back to their homes, hoping that they would be left in peace to plough their fields for the next crop.

As the different families streamed down the long slope, they looked back at the hill. The outline of the rampart and ditch stood out clearly against the sky. The sight made them feel safe. The fort would be there waiting for them to shelter in whenever there was danger.

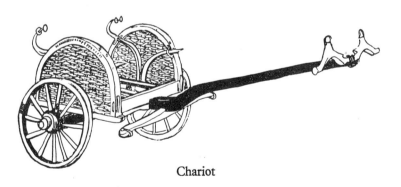

Chariot

THINGS TO DO

1. This book is about three different groups of people. Make a big chart with drawings and explanations showing the different things made by each group and why we connect the first with stone, the second with bronze, and the third with iron.

2. If possible, visit a museum and see how many of the things mentioned in this book you can find. Make drawings to show the different shape of pots, axes and other tools at different periods. Remember to label each drawing Stone, Bronze or Iron Age.

3. Find out from the Ordnance Survey map of your district if there are any places near where prehistoric people lived. If so, visit them and find out whether they were inhabited in the first, second or third period (or possibly all three). Write an imaginary story about the people who lived in these places.

4. If possible, visit Avebury and Stonehenge. In each, try to follow out the whole plan. At Avebury look for the West Kennet Avenue. At Stonehenge notice the long and round barrows dotted over the downs for miles round.

5. Paint an imaginary picture of: flint-mining (page 15); traders from Denmark (page 34); the fight at the fort (page 70).

6. Make a book comparing ways of living in prehistoric Britain with ours today. Arrange it under headings such as houses, clothes, cooking, tools, farming, etc., and show the contrasts by drawings.

7. Try your hand at making things in the ways described in this book, e.g. a flint scraper (page 6), a clay pot (page 9), a stone axe in a wooden handle (page 23). Try spinning and weaving (page 32), and cooking a stew in the way described on page 30.

8. To discuss in class:
    (i) How did discoveries spread from one group to another?
    (ii) Why do people make progress? Do we progress faster than these early people?
    (iii) Why and how did trade begin? How did people pay for things without money?

86

HOW DO WE KNOW ALL THIS?

(1) *Archaeologists* know that these people lived in the ditches because they have found the remains of their fires and meals in them.

(2) The skeleton of a dog was found in the ditch at Windmill Hill camp, in Wiltshire, and at other places too. That is how we know that these farmers used dogs, and what the dogs looked like.

(3) All the bones that archaeologists have dug up at the camps are of young animals.

(4) We know this because some pots have the impression of a mat underneath, made when the clay was wet.

(5) When the pot was fired, the grains of corn were burnt up, leaving a little pit in the side of the pot. Archaeologists make plaster casts from these pits, and can tell from them whether the farmers grew wheat, oats, barley, or rye.

(6) These axes were made of granite, which has sparkling crystals in it.

(7) Archaeologists call patterns made with a loop of cord 'maggot' decoration, because each pattern looks like a maggot.

(8) Archaeologists have found the bones of these creatures, so we know that they lived in Britain then, even though they do not live here now.

(9) Archaeologists have cut down trees with Neolithic axes, and it takes about ten minutes to fell a tree about eight inches thick.

(10) Soot from the miners' lamps has been seen on the chalky roofs of galleries in the flint-mines at Grimes Graves, near Brandon, in Suffolk.

(11) The bones of bats have been found in the flint-mines.

(12) The joints of the bones of many Neolithic people have little knobs in them, which show that they suffered much pain from rheumatism.

(13) Archaeologists have found the pollen of plants and trees that grew long ago in peat formed in bogs that were once lakes. Pollen blew into the water, and was preserved. Under a microscope the pollen of different plants and trees can be sorted out.

(14) Archaeologists have made fields as they think Neolithic people did. They have also seen how people in some parts of Europe still make fields by burning woods. That is how we know about this Neolithic farming.

(15) Apple pip 'impressions' have been found pots : see (5).

(16) There may have been a big ceremony, a kind of funeral 'service', but we do not know what it was like.

(17) If you visit the West Kennet tomb, near Avebury, in Wiltshire, you will see that this stone *was* moved.

(18) Archaeologists have found these cooking-holes. Some have whole pots in them, which proves they were used for cooking. Stones, cracked by heat, are also found in the holes, which are about one foot deep.

(19) Wooden spindles decayed, but clay spindle-whorls have been found in the houses of long ago.

(20) The wooden posts of the loom decayed, but archaeologists have found pairs of holes inside some huts. The holes are filled with black, rotted wood, and are called 'post-holes'.

(21) We know that these people used heddles because one piece of cloth was found with the same mistake repeated many times, until the weaver noticed it and re-tied the heddles.

(22) Pieces of woollen cloth and linen have been found by archaeologists, but only very small pieces because mostly cloth, like wood, decays in the earth.

(23) These beads are made of a kind of glass, called 'faience', and were made in Egypt about 1400 B.C.

(24) Pendants like this were made in Crete. You will see that some of the traders' possessions came from a very long way away, if you look for Crete and Egypt on a map.

(25) Buttons like this were made of jet, from Yorkshire, or sometimes of amber from Denmark. They were sewn on from behind, and the holes were hidden.

(26) Archaeologists think that these woollen caps were imitations of the fur hats Danish people wore before they learned how to weave.

(27) Complete costumes worn by men and women have been found in Denmark. The people were buried in hollowed-out oak-tree coffins, and water happened to collect in the burial mound, or barrow. This water preserved the clothes remarkably: see (22).

(28) Flat axes were decorated with different patterns according to the place where they were made. So archaeologists are able to pick out an Irish axe in a Danish museum.

(29) The first metal-workers in Sumeria (Iraq) discovered that a little tin added to copper makes it tougher and easier to use.

(30) These post-holes have been found at Avebury: see (20).

(31) When archaeologists dug up (excavated) Avebury, they found many holes, filled with different-coloured earth, where the stones of the first temple had once stood. These 'stone-holes' were arranged in three circles.

(32) This is the West Kennet Avenue. You will see some stones still standing if you go to Avebury.

(33) This is now called the 'Sanctuary', and stands on top of Overton Hill. The post-holes are marked by concrete posts to show you how big it was.

(34) This is called the 'Heel' Stone.

(35) Archaeologists have found these stone-holes. They became filled up gradually by earth of a slightly different colour from the rest of the ground.

(36) Stonehenge is such an elaborate temple that one clever man must have worked out the plan. It is a little bit like stone buildings made in Greece, about 1400 B.C., and some archaeologists think that a man from Greece may have helped to plan Stonehenge.

(37) This is called 'mortice and tenon' jointing, usually used to join wood. It is strange that it was used to join stones. We do not know how the lintels were put on top of the stones.

(38) Only one of these remains. It is called the 'Altar Stone'.

(39) Because of this, archaeologists think that Stonehenge was built by people who worshipped the sun as a god.

(40) These holes are now called the X and Y holes on plans of Stonehenge.

(41) The carving of a Greek (Mycenaean) dagger was accidentally found on one of the stones by an archaeologist who was taking a photograph of something else! If you look carefully on all the stones, you will see some carvings of flat axes.

(42) Amber.

(43) Archaeologists have found remains of a house like this at Little Woodbury in Wiltshire. Although nothing showed above the ground, archaeologists found out what shape it had been by uncovering the post-holes : see (20).

(44) These were gods of the Britons who fought the Romans, and later of the Welsh people, who wrote down stories about them in the Middle Ages. The Early Iron Age people were Celts, like the Britons and Welsh, and we think they worshipped the same gods, although they did not know how to write down the stories.

(45) The weather was colder and wetter then than it is now, and many parts of Britain were covered with oak forest full of tangled, damp undergrowth.

(46) Remains of buns like these were found at the Glastonbury Lake Village in Somerset.

(47) The buns found at Glastonbury were put under a microscope. This showed what they were made of.

(48) A lot of burnt corn has been found at Early Iron Age farms.

(49) These people made salt from sea-water by heating bricks and throwing sea-water over them when they were hot.

(50) This story was written down in Ireland in the Middle Ages, but we think it was told for hundreds of years before it was written down.

(51) Just before Julius Caesar visited Britain, in 55 and 54 B.C., the Belgae invaded South-east Britain. They were the first people in Britain to use the potter's wheel for making clay pots.

(52) Traders who lived in Yorkshire used to bury important people in chariots. Although the wooden parts rotted away, archaeologists have been able to reconstruct them from the metal parts.

GLOSSARY

This is a list of special words. If the word you want to know is not here, look for it in your dictionary.

amber: yellow substance, really a kind of gum which has hardened, often made into necklaces or ornaments.

adze: sharp knife used by a carpenter.

antler: long branching horn of a deer.

archaeologist: person who finds out about early people by digging up their houses, graves, etc.

barrow: large mound of earth marking a burying-place.

boss: knob.

bronze: mixture of copper and tin.

bushel: measure of corn.

cauldron: large pot used for cooking over an open fire.

chaff: tough husks covering the grain of corn.

chariot: light, fast carts, often used in fighting.

clan: tribe.

coulter: the part of a plough that digs deep into the soil.

crucible: clay pot in which metals are melted.

fibre: thread or thin stringy substance.

fine-grained: made up of small particles.

flail: wooden bar tied to a long handle used for beating the grains of corn out of the husks.

flint: hard rock which can be made into simple tools and weapons.

fungus: mushrooms and toadstools and the like.

haft: handle.

halberd: long spear.

heddle: rod that picks out the alternate threads in a loom so that the *shuttle* may be passed between them.

to lash: to tie very firmly.

linch-pin: pin used to fix a wheel on the axle.

lintel: whatever lies flat across the tops of uprights, as in the top of a doorway.

loom: wooden framework on which cloth is made.

maul: heavy stone hammer.

molten: melted.

mouldboard: curved plate in a plough which turns over the soil.

ore: rock which contains some metal.

palisade: high wall made of split tree-trunks.

plantain: wild plant, often grows as a weed in lawns.

ploughshare: part of the plough which breaks up the soil.

pyrites: specks of metals that can be seen in a lump of *ore*.

quern: simple hand mill made of stone for grinding corn.

rampart: wall of earth built to fortify a camp or building.

sapling: young tree.

sarsens: large grey blocks of stone found scattered on chalk-lands.

sceptre: short stick carried as a sign of authority.

scrub: land covered with low bushes and coarse weeds.

scythe: tool with a large curved blade for cutting grass.

shaft: deep hole sunk into the ground.

sheath: case for a sword or dagger.

shuttle: tool used to weave thread through the *warp*.

sinew: thin tough strip which joins a muscle to a bone.

to smelt: to melt *ore* so that the metal may be separated from it.

to spin: to twist wool or fibre into a long thin thread.

spindle: piece of wood round which wool was spun.

spindle-whorl: clay weight fixed on one end of a spindle.

thong: strip of leather.

to thresh: to separate the grains of corn from the *chaff*.

warp: threads hanging down the loom through which thread was woven to make cloth.

to weave: to make cloth by intertwining cross-threads with warp-threads.

wheelwright: man who makes wheels.

willow herb: tall bright pink flower, often grows on bomb sites and waste ground.

to winnow: to separate the grains of corn from the *chaff*.

yoke: wooden collar for harnessing oxen.

NEW STONE AGE
□ Flint Mines.
△ Camps.
⟠ Stone axe factories.
● Long barrows.

BRONZE AGE
✛ Sanctuaries.

IRON AGE
⊙ Homes.
▲ Hill forts.

Cairnapple Hill

Keswick
Langdale Pike

Cashtal yn Ard

Arbor Low

Graig Llwyd

R. Severn

R. Trent

Grimes Graves

Pen Dinas

Hunsbury

Bredon Hill

Tinkinswood

Hetty Peglers Tump

Lanhill   Avebury
Oldbury Cas.   Windmill Hill
R. Thames
Stony Littleton
Little Woodbury
West Kennet

Glastonbury   Stonehenge   Trundle   Cissbury
Ham Hill   Caburn

Hembury   Maiden
Castle   Whitehawk

Chysauster
Trencrom

0   50   100
Miles

H.S.W.

Prehistoric Britain